Mr Tickle just loves tickling people. The most people he'd ever tickled in one day was nineteen - until one day he set off for town. Could he beat his own tickling record?

I JUST CAN'T HELP IT

as told to Roger Hargreaves

© Mrs Roger Hargreaves 1985
Printed and published 1991 under licence from Price Stern Sloan Inc.,
Los Angeles. All rights reserved.
Published in Great Britain by World International Publishing Limited,
An Egmont Company, Egmont House, P.O.Box 111, Great Ducie Street,
Manchester M60 3BL. Printed in DDR. ISBN 0 7498 0102 6

A CIP catalogue record for this book is available from the British Library

Hello! I'm Mr Tickle.

Last Monday, when I woke up, I yawned and stretched my arms.

And that's some stretch!

My left arm stretched right out of my bedroom window at one side, and my right arm stretched right out of my bedroom window at the other side!

I felt a little hungry, so do you know what I did?

I reached out, and opened the bedroom door, and reached downstairs into the kitchen, and took out some cornflakes, and poured them into a bowl, and put some milk on them, and brought them back upstairs to me in bed.

Breakfast in bed.

Lovely!

Whoops!

No spoon!

So I sent my arm back downstairs again.

It was a beautiful Monday morning.

The sun was shining, the birds were singing, and to me it looked very much like a tickling sort of a day.

I love to tickle!

I suppose that's why I'm called what I'm called!

Just then there was a knock at the door downstairs.

I peeped out of the bedroom window.

It was the postman.

I grinned a grin.

And I reached out through the bedroom window, and...

TICKLETICKLETICKLETICKLE!

The postman couldn't stop laughing!

"Oh, stop it! Stop it!" he spluttered, dropping all his letters.

I went downstairs, and opened the door.

"Oh, Mr Tickle," the postman gasped. "You are a one!"

I helped him to pick up his letters, and off he went.

I decided to go into town.

On the way, I happened to pass Yawn Cottage.

And you know who happens to live in Yawn Cottage, don't you?

That's right.

Mr Lazy!

And there he was.

In the garden.

In a hammock.

Fast asleep.

Snoring!

Over the hedge went my right arm.

Towards his nose!

Incidentally, my right arm is my best tickling arm.

I just thought you'd like to know.

TICKLETICKLETICKLETICKLE!

He woke up in mid snore.

I quickly pulled my arm back over the hedge.

Mr Lazy looked around.

"It must have been a fly," he grunted.

And went straight back to sleep.

Snore!

Now for the two-arm tickle!

One to the nose.

And one to the tummy!

TICKLETICKLETICKLETICKLE!

Oh, what fun!

Leaving Mr Lazy laughing long and loudly in his heaving hammock, I went on my way.

What a Monday it was turning out to be. Only ten o'clock, and two tickles already!

The third was just three minutes away.

Little Miss Neat. In her garden.

Hanging out the washing.

This book is called *I just can't help it*.

And it's true.

TICKLETICKLETICKLETICKLE!

And one for luck.

TICKLE!

And so the day went on.

I tickled Mr Greedy in the middle of lunch.

I tickled Mr Fussy in a phone box.

I tickled Miss Sunshine in the supermarket.

I tickled Mr Bump until he fell over.

I tickled Mr Chatterbox until he stopped talking.

I tickled Mr Forgetful until he remembered.

I tickled Mr Muddle magnificently.

I tickled Miss Bossy beautifully.

I tickled Mr Silly superbly.

I even tickled Miss Plump perfectly.

Now, the most people that I had ever tickled in one day before was nineteen.

How many had there been today?

I counted them.

One two three four five six seven eight nine ten eleven twelve thirteen!

Thirteen really terrific tickles!

Was I going to beat my record?

The answer was waiting for me around the corner!

A bus queue!

Mr Happy standing behind Miss Giggles standing behind Mr Strong standing behind Miss Naughty standing behind Mr Funny standing behind Miss Helpful.

I quietly joined the end of the queue.

And, when the bus came, I quietly got on.

I sat at the back.

And there, in front of me, were:

Mr Happy
and Miss Giggles
and Mr Strong
and Miss Naughty
and Mr Funny
and Miss Helpful.

TICKLETICKLETICKLETICKLETICKLE!

How many was that?

Fourteen fifteen sixteen seventeen eighteen nineteen!

NINETEEN!

Whoopee!

I had equalled my record!

I got off the bus feeling quite excited.

Just one more!

That's all I needed.

Just one more!

It was getting dark by now.

There was no one around.

Just one more!

Just one more!

And then. Ho, ho.

I spied a tiny figure coming towards me.

"Hello, Mr Tickle," said my friend Mr Small. "Have you had a nice day?"

"The day," I chuckled, "isn't over yet!"

And I reached out my best tickling arm.

You remember which one that is, don't you?

TICKLE!

I'd done it!

I'd done it!

TWENTY REALLY TERRIFIC TICKLES!

TWENTY!

Well. As it was Mr SMALL.

Nineteen and a half!